ROOTED

In Truth

ROOTED *In Truth*

A WRITER'S GUIDE TO FINDING, FACING, AND TELLING YOUR STORY

This book is a companion reflection to the memoir Resilient Roots.

Published by Halaina

First Edition

ISBN: 979-8-9945367-2-8

Cover design by Halaina

Interior design by Halaina

Printed in the United States of America

Dedication

To the roots that held me
when everything shifted,
and to the light
that never left.

Epigraph

Some stories don't begin when you start writing.
They begin the moment you finally decide to remember.

Table of Contents

Dedication i
Epigraph...iii
Introduction vii

PART I – The Seed..1

Planting the Seed..1
Weight of Memory 5
First Page Fear 11
Your Voice & Restraint...15

PART II – The Soil...21

Where Work Begins 23
Scenes vs. Stories 29
Child Inside the Adult...33
Structure Reveals Itself.......................................37

PART III – The Pruning...43

The Real Work..45
Cutting the Excess 51
Simplicity is Strength...55
Chapter Rhythm...59
When a Chapter Ends 63

PART IV – The Bloom..67

First Finished Draft 69
The Long Walk 73
Preparing the Manuscript 79
The Technical Maze 85
Covers, Titles & Identity 93
Publishing the Book 99
Pressing "Publish" 105

PART V — The Garden 109

Letting Go 111
What Changes 117
Every Story Has Roots 121
What Remains 125
About the Author 131

Introduction

Most people don't struggle because they don't have a story. They struggle because they don't know where to begin.

When I finished writing *Resilient Roots*, I believed the journey was complete. The story had finally been told. Years of memories had been shaped into chapters, and the quiet work of writing had grown into a book that now lived beyond my desk.

But something unexpected began to happen. People started asking questions—not only about the story itself, but about how the books came into existence. They wanted to know what inspired *Resilient Roots*, how *One Land, Two* Sides evolved, and what led me to write *Rooted in Truth.*

Those conversations made me realize the journey was never only about publishing books. It was about the experiences, reflections, and lessons that shaped each one along the way.

How did you remember everything?

How did you begin writing?

How did you keep going when the story became difficult?

Again and again, I heard the same sentence:

"I have a story too... but I don't know how to write it."

Those conversations stayed with me.

This book is my answer to them.

It isn't a textbook. It isn't a formula. It's an honest account of what it took to write these books—the doubts, the resistance, the late nights, the moments I almost stopped, and the ones that kept me going. Every chapter reflects something I truly lived through along the way.

If you have a story you haven't written yet, this is for you. Not because your path will look exactly like mine, but because it will look like yours—and this might help you trust it.

Every story has roots.

Yours is already there.

This book is about learning to follow it.

PART I — The Seed

Planting the Seed

It didn't begin at a desk. It began in the rain.

I was alone in the motorhome, parked by the lakeside at a campsite that felt quieter than I expected—the kind of quiet that doesn't distract you, but leaves you with yourself. The rain had been falling long enough for the air to change, hitting the roof in a steady rhythm while the smell of damp earth slipped through the cracks of the windows, mixing with the faint scent of coffee gone cold beside me.

There was no movement, just space—the kind that doesn't fill itself. I sat in the captain's chair, looking out over the lake as the rain tapped against the glass, breaking across the water in soft, uneven circles before disappearing. Camping had a way of doing that, slowing everything down long enough for me to hear my own thoughts.

And then it came back.

"You should write your story."

I had heard it before, many times, and ignored it for years. But sitting there, it didn't pass. It stayed.

I shifted in my seat, almost like I could move away from it just by moving, but nothing changed. The campground stayed quiet. The thought remained.

I didn't make a decision. I reached for my laptop and sat in bed, the sound of rain and pinecones tapping softly against the roof. My fingers hovered over the keys longer than they should have. The first line came slower than I expected, then another.

There was no plan, no outline, no thought about where it was going. I didn't reread. I didn't fix anything. I just kept typing, letting whatever came out stay there.

That was the first time I gave it somewhere to go—not the book, just the act of letting it leave me and land somewhere else. For years, I had held it there. That night, I didn't.

It didn't feel like a beginning. It felt small, quiet, something that could easily be forgotten by morning. But it wasn't. Because once it was on the page, it wasn't only mine anymore.

You think it's just a few lines, something temporary, something you may or may not come back to—but it's not. It's the moment you stop holding it in.

The rain slowed sometime later, softening until it barely made a sound against the roof. I closed what I had written and set it aside.

The next morning, when I had a quiet moment, I reached for it again—not because I had a system, not because I had a plan, but because something in me knew where to go.

That's how it began—not as a book, not as a plan, not even as a decision, just something I finally stopped pushing away.

Your Thought

Stories don't begin when you decide to write. They begin the moment you stop ignoring them. You don't need a plan, structure, or clarity to start—you need attention, honesty, and one small moment you don't dismiss. You don't need the whole story. You just need to let the first piece exist.

Carry This

Sit somewhere quiet. Open a blank document. Write one memory. Don't organize it. Don't reread while writing. Stop before you overthink it. Come back the next day.

What Stayed

You don't begin with a book. You begin with a moment. And the moment you give it a place to exist—you've already started.

Weight of Memory

I thought I was going to write what happened. That was the plan—sit down, start at the beginning, and move forward, one memory after another until it was all there.

It didn't work that way.

The first time I opened what I had written, I expected it to feel familiar, like something I had already lived through and understood. It didn't. I read a few lines and stopped—not because they were wrong, but because they were closer than I expected.

The room came back first. Not as an idea, but as a place.

I had thought memory would be steady, something I could reach for like a shelf where the past had been stored, waiting to be placed onto the page. But memory didn't come when I asked for it. It came on its own.

Sometimes it arrived quietly while I was writing about something small—a room, a street, the sound of voices through an open window—and something else surfaced behind it, clearer than I expected. It wasn't loud. It had always been there.

I leaned back, my hands pulling away from the keyboard. A courtyard. Stone steps worn smooth by years of footsteps. My mother's voice moving from room to room. The smell of bread rising somewhere nearby.

Those moments didn't feel like I was searching for them. They felt like they had been waiting beneath the surface for me to slow down enough to notice them.

And even when I moved past that first moment, it didn't become easier the way I expected. There were moments I had to stop—not because I didn't know what came next, but because I felt it too clearly. The scenes didn't stay on the page. They came back with me.

I had to decide if I was willing to stay there long enough to write them the way they actually were. Not the way I remembered them later, but the way they felt when I was inside them—the walls, the light, the way sound moved through the room. It didn't feel like I was writing about it. It felt like I had stepped back into it.

Other times, memory came differently. Not as images, but as sensation. A tightening in my chest before I understood why. A silence that felt heavier than it should. The sharp rhythm of boots striking pavement.

Those were harder to stay in—not because I didn't recognize them, but because I did. Too quickly.

I would close the laptop, sit there longer than I needed to, then open it again. The next memory didn't come in order. It came in pieces—a sound before a face, a feeling before a scene, the echo of something before I could see where I was.

At first, I tried to organize it, to make it clean, to make it make sense. But every time I forced it, it stopped. The moment would disappear.

I stopped forcing it.

I wrote what came, even when it didn't connect, even when it didn't make sense yet. And the more I stayed with it, the more it opened. One moment led to another. A sentence brought back a room. The room brought back a day. The day uncovered something I hadn't thought about in years.

Some memories stayed longer, clear enough to follow. Others didn't. They came as pressure, not images. Not every memory came back fully. Sometimes there were gaps. Sometimes what remained was only the feeling—the weight of a moment more than the details around it.

I stopped trying to make it complete.

I wrote what I could see. What I could feel. Until something began to take shape.

The memories didn't just return—they started connecting. A moment I wrote one night led into another I hadn't thought about in years. Something small opened something bigger. Not all at once, but enough to follow.

Moments that once felt isolated began to reveal what had always been beneath them. A pattern. A thread. Something that had been there all along.

I stopped trying to tell the story and started watching it form.

This wasn't random. It wasn't just pieces of the past coming back. There was something underneath it, holding it together. What I had carried for years without understanding began to make sense in a way it never had before. Not softer. Not easier. Just clearer.

That's when writing changed.

It stopped being something I was trying to get through and became something I had to stay with. Because once you see it like that, you don't go back to writing the way you thought you would.

You follow it.

One piece at a time.

Your Thought

Memory doesn't work in order—and your story doesn't need to either. You don't need a timeline, a clear beginning, or a perfect structure to start. Memory moves through moments, emotion, and connection, and if you try to control it too early, you stop it. The story reveals itself after you begin, not before.

Carry This

Start with what stays. Not the beginning—just the moment that returns most clearly. Let it come without forcing it into order. Follow where it leads, even if it doesn't make sense yet. And when it feels heavy, pause—but don't leave it behind. Come back to it. Because what keeps returning is usually what matters.

What Stayed

You don't build your story in order. You uncover it. And the more you allow it to come as it is—the more honest it becomes.

First Page Fear

The hardest part wasn't writing the story. It was starting.

I had written before—small pieces, moments that came out without much thought. But this felt different. This time, I knew what I was sitting down to face.

I remember the night clearly. The house was quiet in a way that made every small sound stand out—the faint hum of something running in the background, the soft shift of air moving through the room. Everything else was still.

I sat down at the computer and opened a blank document. The screen lit up, bright against the dark around it.

I didn't type.

My hands rested on the keyboard, but they didn't move. The cursor blinked. On. Off. Waiting.

And then it came. Not the story. The doubt.

Halaina

Who am I to do this?

It wasn't loud. It didn't need to be. It had been there the whole time, just waiting for me to notice it. I leaned back slightly, my fingers pulling away from the keys.

For a moment, I looked at the screen like it was asking something from me I wasn't sure I could give. Because writing a book is not the same as thinking about one. Thinking is safe. You can shape it, adjust it, walk away from it whenever you want. But writing fixes it in place. And that changes everything.

Who will read this? What if I remember something wrong? What if I say something that hurts someone? What if I start and can't finish?

I didn't answer them. I just sat there with them, letting them take up space. Because the truth was, I didn't have answers.

I had the same life I had always had—the same hands that worked behind a salon chair all day, the same routine, the same responsibilities waiting for me in the morning. Nothing about me had suddenly changed just because I opened a blank page.

And that's what made it harder.

There was no moment where I became a writer. No shift. No permission. Just me, sitting there, deciding whether I was going to do it or not.

I looked at the screen again. The cursor was still blinking. Still waiting.

Something in me moved. Not loudly. Not all at once. Just enough. The same feeling I had in the motorhome. That quiet push I couldn't ignore anymore.

The story wasn't going anywhere. Avoiding it wasn't making it smaller. It was only keeping it inside.

I leaned forward again and placed my hands back on the keyboard.

This time, I didn't wait for it to feel right.

I pressed the first key.

One word.

Then another.

Your Thought

Starting doesn't come from confidence. It comes from willingness. The doubt doesn't disappear before you begin—it stays, asking questions you may not have answers to. But something shifts the moment you stop waiting for certainty and begin anyway.

Carry This

When you sit in front of a blank page, don't wait for the right feeling to arrive. It may not. Let the doubt be there without trying to resolve it, and begin anyway. Start with one word, then another. You don't need to know where it's going—you only need to give it somewhere to begin.

What Stayed

You don't start because you're ready.

You start because you stop waiting.

Your Voice & Restraint

I believed I needed to sound like a writer. That was the mistake.

When I first started putting real pages together, I paid more attention to how the sentences looked than to how they felt. I had read enough books to know what "good writing" sounded like—the words polished, the sentences carrying weight, everything intentional. So I tried to do the same. I would write a sentence, then go back and adjust it, adding more, stretching it, changing simple words into ones that sounded stronger.

It looked better on the page.

But something was off.

I could feel it when I read it back. The sentences didn't move the way they should—they sat there, heavy, like they were trying too hard to prove something. I remember stopping in the middle of a paragraph and just staring at it. It didn't sound like me. Not the way I spoke, not the way I thought—just something I believed it was supposed to be.

I leaned back in my chair and let it sit there for a minute. The room was quiet, but my mind wasn't. I kept rereading the same lines, hoping they would settle into place. They didn't.

I deleted them. Not all at once, just a few lines at a time, until what was left felt almost too simple—shorter sentences, clearer words, nothing added just to make it sound better. At first, it felt like I was taking something away, lowering the quality instead of improving it. But it sounded like me. The version I already was.

I had been using that voice every day without thinking about it—behind the salon chair, talking to someone who wasn't looking for perfect words, just real ones. I never stopped to make a sentence sound impressive. I asked questions the way they came and answered the same way, and people understood me. They trusted it because it wasn't trying to be anything else.

Sitting there at the computer, I realized I had been doing the opposite on the page—trying to replace something that was already working. I paused. I didn't try to sound like anything. I just wrote the way I would say it.

The difference was immediate. The sentences moved, the memories stayed closer, and nothing felt forced.

Your voice is not something you build. It's something you stop interfering with. The more you try to shape it into something better, the further it moves away from you. And the moment you let it come through the way it naturally does, the writing begins to carry itself—not because it's perfect, but because it's real.

At first, I explained too much. I didn't trust the moment to stand on its own, so I stayed in it longer than I needed to, adding meaning and clarifying what was already there. When I read it back, it felt heavier—not stronger, just overworked. The moment was still there, but something had been placed on top of it, softening what should have been sharp.

I started noticing it while I was writing. A scene would return clearly—the room, the people in it, the way something shifted without being said—and instead of leaving it alone, I would step in and explain what I understood now, why it mattered, and what it led to. Every time I did that, the scene lost something. It stopped feeling immediate and became distant, like I was standing outside it instead of being inside it.

I pulled back. I wrote the moment the way it happened and let it end where it naturally ended. A conversation behind a closed door. A shift in someone's voice when I entered the room. The way people moved when something wasn't right. I left it there.

When I read those moments back, they held more—not because I added anything, but because I didn't. The meaning was already inside them. It was present in the way the moment unfolded.

The more I trusted that, the less I interfered. I stopped guiding every emotion. I stopped trying to make sure the reader understood exactly what I had come to understand over time. Instead, I allowed the scene to carry its own weight.

That's what restraint became for me—not holding anything back, but knowing when the moment had said enough and having the discipline to leave it there.

Your Thought

Your voice isn't something you create. It's something you stop trying to improve. And the moment you trust it, the writing becomes clearer, stronger, and more honest.

Carry This

Write the way you already speak. Not the polished version or the improved version—the real one. Let the moment arrive as it is and resist the urge to explain it afterward. If it's clear, leave it. If it lands, move on. What feels simple is often what holds the most truth.

What Stayed

Your voice was never missing. You were just speaking over it.

PART II — The Soil

Where Work Begins

Finding my voice didn't make the writing easier. If anything, it made it more real. Because once I stopped trying to sound like someone else, there was nothing left to hide behind. It was just me—and the page.

The page was still empty.

I used to think writing would come naturally once I understood what I wanted to say. That the story would carry itself. That I would sit down and it would move.

It didn't happen like that.

Life didn't change just because I decided to write a book. The salon stayed full. My phone kept ringing. Appointments filled every space they could. Women came in with their stories, their voices, their lives that didn't slow down. Neither did mine.

By the time I got home, my body felt it. My feet carried the weight of the day. My hands ached in that quiet, familiar way that comes from years of holding scissors, combs, brushes. Dinner still needed to be made. Messages still needed answers. The next day was already waiting.

Writing didn't appear in the middle of that.

I made a decision early on. The book would not wait for life to slow down. Life was not going to slow down. So I found the one window that belonged to no one else—after the salon closed, after the house quieted, after everything that needed doing had been done. Late. Later than I should have been awake. I brewed coffee I didn't need and sat down anyway.

Some nights I wrote for an hour. Some nights for twenty minutes. Some nights I opened the laptop and stared at it and closed it again. But I came back the next night. And the one after that.

Most nights, that space came late—when the house finally settled and the noise dropped low enough for me to hear myself again. I would open the laptop and sit there.

Sometimes the words came. A memory would return clear enough to follow. The courtyard in Ramallah would rise again—the warmth of stone under my feet, voices carrying across balconies, something I could step into and stay with. Those nights felt easier. Not effortless. Just moving.

Other nights were different. I would sit there and nothing would come. The screen stayed still, the cursor blinking the same way it always had—on, off, waiting.

And the doubt would try to find its way back in. Maybe I don't have this in me. Maybe I've already said what I can say. Maybe this isn't going to become anything.

I let those thoughts sit. I didn't try to fix them. I just stayed.

That became the difference. Not whether the writing was good. Not whether it flowed. But whether I stayed long enough for something to happen.

Some nights, nothing did. Some nights, all I had was a few lines—sometimes just a paragraph before I closed the laptop and let it go for the night.

But I came back. Not perfectly. Not on a schedule that always made sense. But enough.

The book wasn't being built in big moments. It was being built in small returns—a sentence that stayed, something written on a night when I didn't feel like writing at all.

That's what held it together. Not inspiration. Not waiting for the right mood.

The story didn't rush. It grew. Slow. Uneven. Sometimes quiet enough that I wondered if anything was happening at all.

But when I looked back, it was there. More than there. It was forming.

Writing doesn't wait for your life to clear space. It happens inside it—between exhaustion and the decision to keep going anyway.

And most days, that decision felt small. Almost unnoticeable. Just sitting down. Opening the page. Staying there long enough for something to move.

Your Thought

Writing doesn't require perfect conditions. It requires return. You don't need more time, energy, or motivation to begin—you need to sit down anyway, stay even when nothing comes, and come back again the next day. That's how books are written, not all at once, but in small, consistent moments.

Carry This

Choose a small window of time and return to it consistently. Sit down even when you don't feel like it and write something, even if it's only a sentence. Let imperfect writing exist without trying to fix it right away, and stop before you burn out so you can come back again. The habit isn't built in one session—it's built in showing up, again and again.

What Stayed

You don't need more time. You need a willingness to return. Because writing isn't built on inspiration—it's built on showing up.

Scenes vs. Stories

At first, I thought I needed to explain my life. I would sit down and move quickly through events—the way I might speak them out loud. This happened. Then this. Then this. Years passed in a paragraph. Important moments appeared briefly, then disappeared just as fast. Nothing was wrong with it, but something was missing.

I could read it back and understand what had happened. But I couldn't feel it.

That's when I noticed the difference—between telling something and being inside it.

I went back and slowed down. Not everything. Just certain moments that stayed longer than the others. A room. A voice. A moment that didn't leave as quickly as the rest. The memory didn't feel like information anymore. It felt like a place.

I could see it more clearly—the way light moved across the floor, the way sound carried through the space, the small details I had rushed past before.

A courtyard. Stone worn smooth beneath my feet. Voices crossing from one balcony to another.

Those moments didn't need explanation. They held something on their own.

Not every part of a life needs to be told the same way. Some parts move quickly. Others need space. Once I started writing in scenes, I had to understand where a scene actually closed—not where I wanted it to end, but where the experience itself had completed. A scene isn't defined by length or intensity. It's defined by completion. Until that point, it continues.

The ones that stay with you—the ones you can still see, still feel—those are the ones you don't rush. You stay in them long enough for them to unfold.

I started asking myself different questions. Not what happened next—but where was I standing? Who else was there? What could I hear? What could I see?

The answers didn't come as explanations. They came as pieces. A smell. A sound. The way a room felt when no one was speaking.

And slowly, those pieces began to build something fuller.

The more I wrote like that, the more the story changed. It wasn't something I was describing anymore. It was something I was stepping back into.

And when I could see it clearly, I didn't need to say as much.

The moment carried itself.

Not more explanation.

More presence.

A life can hold thousands of memories. But it's the ones you stay in—the ones you allow to fully unfold—that begin to shape the story into something real.

Your Thought

Readers don't connect to information—they connect to experience. When you only tell what happened, they understand it. But when you show what it felt like, they begin to feel it too. And that is where your story becomes real.

Carry This

Begin with a single moment instead of trying to tell everything at once. Place yourself inside it—where you were, who was there, what you could see, hear, and feel. Slow it down and let it unfold naturally, without stepping in to explain it. When the moment is honest, it carries its own meaning.

What Stayed

Your story isn't built from everything that happened. It's built from the moments you choose to stay in.

Child Inside the Adult

When I began writing Resilient Roots, I realized something quickly — I wasn't writing from one place. I was writing from two. The one holding the pen, and the one who had lived it.

The woman sitting at the computer understood things the child never could. I could see the tension around us in Ramallah. I could understand the weight my parents carried, the meaning behind conversations that once felt distant or unclear, the things that had shaped the moments I was now trying to put into words.

But the child didn't know any of that.

She only knew what she could see. A shift in someone's voice. The way a room felt when it went quiet. The way adults looked at each other when they thought no one was paying attention.

That's what stayed with the child. Not explanations. Not context. Just experience.

At first, I tried to explain everything. Fill in the gaps. Make sure it made sense. But every time I did, the moment changed. It lost something. It stopped feeling like it belonged to her — to the child I had been.

I pulled back.

I stayed with what the child would have noticed. The way a door closed harder than usual. The way a conversation stopped when she walked into the room. The way her mother's hands moved faster than normal, even if no one said why.

The child didn't need to understand it to feel it.

That was enough.

The more I trusted that, the clearer the writing became. I didn't need to explain fear. It was already there — in the silence, in the way people moved, in the things that weren't said out loud.

The adult voice didn't disappear. It stayed behind the structure, shaping the story, deciding where it moved and how it held together. But inside the scenes, the adult stepped back. It let the child remain where she was — watching, listening, trying to make sense of a world that didn't explain itself to her.

That's where the truth was. Not in what I understand now as the adult, but in what she experienced then as the child.

And somewhere between those two places, something settled. Not a correction. Not a rewrite. Just a clearer way of seeing it.

The child didn't need to know everything for the story to be complete. She only needed to be honest. And the adult didn't need to take over — only to recognize what had always been there.

That's where the balance lived. Not in choosing one voice over the other, but in letting both exist without one replacing the other.

Because the story was never only one of them. It was both.

Your Thought

You don’t need to explain your story for it to be understood. You need to show it honestly. When you stay inside what you experienced instead of stepping back to explain it, the truth becomes clearer—and often, saying less creates more impact.

Carry This

Return to a moment from your past and stay inside it as you were then. Write from what you knew in that moment, not from what you understand now. Let it unfold through what you saw, heard, and felt, and allow the reader to experience it without explanation.

What Stayed

You don't need to explain everything. The truth is already inside the moment.

Structure Reveals Itself

At first, the pages didn't connect. I wasn't building a book—I was writing whatever came back, one memory at a time. A room. A voice. A moment that stayed longer than the others. I didn't think about where it belonged. I didn't try to organize it. I just wrote it before it disappeared again.

I thought I would need a plan. An outline. Something clear before I started—a way to see the whole book before I wrote the first page. Beginning. Middle. End.

I didn't have that.

I had pieces.

Some days took me back to Ramallah—the courtyard, the stone under my feet, voices crossing between balconies. Other days pulled me somewhere completely different—years later, a different place, a different version of me.

There was no order.

For a while, that felt like a problem. I would look at what I had written and try to make sense of it. Move things around. Line them up the way I thought a story was supposed to go.

But every time I forced it, something didn't sit right.

The pieces didn't hold.

I stopped trying to control it. And I kept writing.

Slowly, something began to happen. Not all at once—just enough to notice. A moment I had written early on connected to something new. A scene from childhood explained something I didn't understand until years later. Things that felt separate weren't separate at all. They were tied together in ways I hadn't recognized before.

Not because I planned it. Because they belonged together.

Certain pieces carried the same weight, the same pull. When I placed them near each other, something opened between them—meaning I hadn't seen before.

That's when the story started to change. It wasn't just memory anymore. It was a pattern.

I could see it in the way certain moments returned more than others, the way some scenes carried more weight—even when they seemed small at the time. I started paying attention to that.

Not every memory needed space. But the ones that wouldn't leave—the ones that came back again and again—those were doing something.

I stayed with them. Let them stretch a little longer on the page. Let them reveal what they were connected to.

The more I did that, the clearer it became.

The story had been there the whole time—not in order, but underneath it, holding everything together.

That's when I stopped looking for structure on the surface and started paying attention to what was underneath—the movement of it, where it was taking me. Childhood. Leaving. Starting over. Losing. Rebuilding.

Those weren't decisions I made at the beginning. They were already there. I just hadn't seen them yet.

I just hadn't stayed with it long enough to recognize the structure.

Once I did, everything started settling into place. Not perfectly. Naturally.

Your Thought

You don't need to know your entire story before you begin. Structure isn't something you build at the start—it's something that reveals itself as you keep going. When you stop trying to control it and allow the pieces to exist as they come, patterns begin to surface. What once felt scattered starts to connect, and slowly, the story begins to take shape on its own.

Carry This

Write without trying to organize everything too soon. Let moments exist on their own, even if they don't make sense yet. Over time, notice what returns—the themes, the memories that won't leave. Place those closer together and see what begins to form. Structure isn't something you force—it's something you recognize after you've written enough to see it.

What Stayed

Your story already has structure. You just have to write enough to see it.

PART III — The Pruning

The Real Work

Some parts of the book came easily. I would sit down, start writing, and the pages would fill before I had time to think. One memory led to another. The story carried itself.

Then it would stop.

Not gradually. Completely.

And sometimes it wasn't the memory that stopped me. It was the question behind it—whether any of this mattered, whether it was something anyone would want to read.

The doubt didn't come once. It returned in different ways, at different points, asking the same thing. Who is this for? Why does it matter?

And each time, the only way forward was the same. To keep writing anyway.

I would be in the middle of a scene when the words slowed, then disappeared altogether. I would sit there, looking at what I had just written, knowing exactly where the memory was going—and not wanting to follow it any further.

It wasn't that I didn't know what came next. I knew. Too clearly.

I could see where it was going, what it was about to open, and what I would have to stay in if I kept going. And I didn't want to go there.

I closed the laptop. Walked away.

Not because the story didn't matter. Because it did.

The chapter about Nicholas was the hardest. I knew it was coming. I had circled around it for weeks—writing other things, letting it sit at the edge of the page without going near it. One night, I finally opened it. I wrote one sentence and stopped. I sat in front of that sentence for twenty minutes before I closed the laptop entirely.

I didn't go back for three days.

When I did, I wrote the next sentence. Then the one after. Not because I had found a way to make it easier. Because I understood by then that easy wasn't what the chapter needed. It needed honesty. And honesty, in that case, required staying in a place I had spent years learning how to leave.

That's when I started to understand what was happening.

The parts that are hardest to write are usually the most important. Not because they're dramatic, but because they're honest.

Some memories don't resist because they're forgotten. They resist because they're still close. Writing brings them back.

And once they're back, you have to decide—whether to stay with it or avoid it.

That's the real work.

Not writing when it's easy. Writing when it isn't.

There were nights I didn't go back to it — nights I let the page sit unfinished because I wasn't ready to stay there longer than I already had.

But I always came back. Not all at once, not forcing it in a single sitting—just enough to move a little further each time. A sentence, then another.

Until the part I wanted to avoid was no longer in front of me—but behind me. Written. Not carried.

The places where the writing stopped weren't weak points in the story. They were the center of it. The moments I struggled to stay in were the ones holding the most weight.

Avoiding them didn't protect the story. It kept it incomplete.

I stopped expecting those parts to be easy. I stopped trying to move through them the same way I moved through everything else. Some scenes required more time, more space, more honesty than I was comfortable with at first.

But once I stayed in them long enough to write them as they were, something shifted.

Not lighter. Stronger.

Because those were the moments that changed everything.

Your Thought

Every writer reaches a point where writing becomes uncomfortable. That isn't something to avoid—it's part of the process. When everything feels easy, it often means you're staying on the surface. The deeper parts of your story are usually found in the places that resist you, the ones that ask you to slow down and stay a little longer than you want to.

Carry This

When you feel the urge to stop, pause long enough to notice why. You don't have to face it all at once—just take a small step forward. Write a sentence, then another. Give yourself space when you need it, but don't leave it completely. The work isn't in forcing your way through—it's in staying with it long enough for something to shift.

What Stayed

The parts you avoid writing are often the parts that make your story real.

Cutting the Excess

While I was writing, everything felt important. Every scene. Every moment. Every line. I had worked to remember it, to bring it back, to put it into words. Nothing felt unnecessary.

I didn't question it then.

That changed when I started reading it back—not as the writer, but as someone moving through it.

That's when I saw it.

Some scenes were staying longer than they needed to. The emotion was already there, but I had written past it—adding more, explaining more, repeating what was already clear.

At first, I didn't want to touch it. Because I remembered what it took to write it.

But that wasn't the question anymore.

The question was simple—does it belong?

I started going through the chapters slowly, not looking for what was good, but for what was repeated. Where the story had already said what it needed to say, and where I had stayed out of attachment instead of purpose.

And once I saw it, I couldn't unsee it.

The extra lines didn't make the story stronger. They blurred it.

I started cutting. Not everything at once—a sentence, a paragraph, sometimes an entire scene that had once felt essential.

I would remove it and read the chapter again, expecting something to feel missing. Most of the time, it didn't.

The moment stood on its own. Clearer. Stronger. More focused.

Because nothing was competing with it anymore.

Some scenes were harder to let go of—not because they didn't belong, but because they were tied to something I had carried for a long time.

I didn't delete them completely. I moved them. Kept them in a separate place—not in the book, but not gone either.

That made it easier to be honest about what the chapter actually needed.

And the more I did it, the more the story changed. It moved faster. Cleaner. The moments that remained held more weight—not because I added anything to them, but because nothing was competing with them anymore.

Editing wasn't asking for more. It was asking for less.

Not removing what mattered—but removing what repeated it.

And once I let go of what didn't belong, the story didn't feel smaller. It felt sharper.

Your Thought

More writing doesn't always make the story stronger. In many cases, it does the opposite. Clarity comes from removing what isn't needed—letting go of repetition, extra explanation, and anything that sits around the moment instead of inside it. When you step back and allow only what truly matters to remain, the story begins to stand on its own.

Carry This

Read your work slowly, as if you're moving through it for the first time. Notice where it lingers too long or repeats something that has already been felt. Stay with what moves the story forward, and trust the moments that already hold meaning. When something doesn't add to it, allow yourself to let it go. The story doesn't weaken—it becomes clearer.

What Stayed

You don't lose your story by cutting. You reveal it.

Simplicity is Strength

At first, I thought more words made the writing stronger. More explanation. More detail. More clarity.

But when I read it back, it felt heavy. Slower. Less clear.

I didn't notice it while I was writing. The pages felt full, complete—like everything needed to be there. But when I started reading it again, I began to see it. The same idea repeated. A feeling introduced, then explained again in a different way. A moment that had already landed, followed by another sentence to make sure it was understood.

At first, I left it. It felt safer that way, like I was protecting the meaning.

But the more I read, the more it stood out. The writing wasn't getting stronger with more words. It was getting slower.

I tested it. I removed one sentence, then read it again, expecting something to feel missing. Most of the time, nothing was.

If anything, it felt clearer. The moment didn't need help. It needed space.

That's when I began looking at the pages differently—not for what could be added, but for what could be removed without changing the meaning.

I started noticing patterns. A sentence explaining what the scene had already shown. A line repeating an emotion already felt. A paragraph circling something instead of moving forward.

I began cutting them. Slowly at first, then with more confidence. And every time I did, the same thing happened.

The writing tightened. The scene held its shape. The emotion stayed—without anything around it softening the edge.

Simplicity wasn't taking anything away. It was revealing what was already working.

The fewer words around a true moment, the more clearly it could be seen.

I stopped trying to make sure the reader understood everything. If the scene was honest, it carried enough. It didn't need to be repeated. It needed to be left as it was.

And once I trusted that, the story changed. It didn't become bigger. It held.

Your Thought

Strong writing isn't about adding more—it's about leaving what matters. When you remove what's unnecessary, the writing becomes clearer, the emotion sharpens, and the story is able to stand without distraction.

Carry This

Approach your writing with the intention to simplify rather than expand. Notice where ideas repeat or where explanation replaces experience. Let go of what doesn't move the story forward, and trust that honest moments can hold their own without needing anything added around them.

What Stayed

The fewer words around a true moment—the more powerful it becomes.

Chapter Rhythm

I didn't notice rhythm while I was writing. I was focused on getting it down—capturing the memory before it slipped away, moving from one moment to the next before I lost it.

The pages grew. But they didn't move the same way.

I only saw it once I started reading it back. Some chapters carried me through without effort. I would move from one scene to the next without stopping, not thinking about structure—just following it.

Others felt heavier. Not because of the content, but because something was holding them there too long.

At first, I thought it was the story—that certain parts were just harder. But that wasn't it. Some of the heaviest moments moved cleanly, while some of the lighter ones dragged.

That's when I started paying attention. Not to what I was saying, but to how it moved—where it slowed, and where it rushed.

I began noticing places where I had stayed too long after the moment had already landed. The scene had done its work, but I kept going—adding more, softening what should have stayed sharp.

I also saw places where I moved too quickly, where a moment that needed space was passed over in a few lines and gone before it had time to settle.

I started adjusting. Not what I said, but how long I stayed.

Sometimes I let a moment breathe, staying in it long enough to see it fully before moving on. Other times I ended it sooner, letting it close where it naturally ended instead of carrying it further than it needed to go.

The more I worked through it, the clearer it became.

The story wasn't just what I was saying. It was how it moved.

That movement changed depending on what the chapter was holding. Some chapters needed space—room for the reader to pause and take in what had just settled. Others needed to stay tight, carrying one moment directly into the next without interruption.

When I treated them the same, the rhythm broke. A chapter built on tension lost its pressure when I gave it too much space. But when I let it move the way it needed to, the weight stayed intact.

The rhythm shifted with what each chapter demanded. Short lines pushed it forward. Longer ones slowed it just enough to stay inside a moment. Breaks gave it space without stopping it completely.

I didn't think about it as rules. I felt it. When it was off, I could hear it. When it was right, I didn't notice it at all.

Rhythm isn't something you force onto a chapter. It's something you recognize once you start listening to how the story is already moving.

And once it settles into place, the reader doesn't stop to think about it. They just keep going.

Your Thought

Your story isn't only shaped by what you write—it's shaped by how it moves. The rhythm of it determines how a reader experiences each moment, where they pause, and where they continue. When that movement feels natural, the story begins to carry itself without effort.

Carry This

Read your writing straight through, not to fix it, but to feel how it moves. Notice where it slows too much or passes too quickly. Give space to the moments that need to breathe, and tighten the ones that linger too long. Let each part unfold at its own pace, and trust that variation is what creates rhythm.

What Stayed

Good writing isn't just clear. It moves.

When a Chapter Ends

At some point, I stopped knowing what else to change. Not because it was perfect, but because I had already changed it too many times.

I would return to the same chapter again and again. Read it slowly. Adjust a sentence. Move a paragraph. Add something I thought was missing, then remove something that suddenly felt unnecessary.

Some days it felt finished. The next day, it didn't.

Nothing obvious was wrong, but I kept looking for something to fix.

That's where it became difficult—not writing it, but knowing when to stop. Because there was always something I could change. A sentence could be tighter. A line could be softer. A moment could be expanded just a little more.

And for a while, I followed that instinct. I kept adjusting it, trying to make it better.

But the more I touched it, the less clear it became. The edges softened. The rhythm shifted. And moments that once landed cleanly began to feel worked over.

That's when I stepped back.

I read it without trying to fix anything, just moving through it the way a reader would. And I could feel it—where it held, where it moved, and where it had already said enough.

The chapter didn't need more work. It needed to be left alone.

I wasn't making it stronger anymore. I was interfering with what was already working.

I stopped asking how to improve it and started asking something simpler.

Does it hold? Does the moment land? Can I move forward from here without needing more?

When the answer was yes, I left it—not because it was perfect, but because it was complete.

That's when the decision became clear. A chapter doesn't end when there's nothing left to change. It ends when you recognize that changing it again won't make it better—and you're willing to let it stand.

Your Thought

A chapter doesn't end when there's nothing left to change—it ends when changing it no longer makes it better. Perfection can keep you circling the same page, but completion is what allows the story to move forward.

Carry This

Read your work without trying to fix it. Move through it as a whole and notice how it feels rather than focusing on every small detail. When you find yourself adjusting things without real change, it may be a sign to step back and let it stand. At some point, the work isn't improved by more effort—it's strengthened by leaving it as it is.

What Stayed

Finished is better than perfect.

PART IV — The Bloom

First Finished Draft

The last sentence didn't feel the way I expected it to.

I thought it would feel bigger. Clearer. Like something had finally landed.

Instead, I just sat there with the cursor blinking beneath it—and nothing left to write.

For months, there had always been something waiting. Another page. Another memory. Another chapter I hadn't reached yet. Even on the days I didn't want to sit down, I knew where I was going next.

Now there was nowhere left to go.

The story was there. From beginning to end.

I didn't move right away. I just sat in it, letting it settle, trying to understand what had just happened.

Because finishing it didn't feel like an ending. It felt different.

At first, there was a sense of relief. Not loud—just steady. I had stayed with it through the nights when nothing came, through the moments I wanted to stop, and through the parts I didn't want to write but did anyway.

Somehow, it had carried all the way through. And that part felt real.

But it didn't stay there.

Something else came with it—quiet at first, then clearer.

Now it was complete. And that changed everything.

As long as it was unfinished, it stayed with me. It was still forming, still shifting, still something I could adjust without anyone ever seeing it.

Now it existed as a whole. And that meant it could be read.

That's where the fear came in.

Not about writing it—but about what came after.

I remember opening the manuscript again and reading it from the beginning, this time knowing there was nothing left to add.

Some parts felt exactly right. Others showed me where the work wasn't done yet. But none of that changed the one thing that mattered.

It was there.

Everything I had carried and worked through was no longer in pieces. It had taken shape.

That's what finishing the first draft actually is.

It isn't the end of the work. It's the moment the story becomes real enough to face.

And once it reaches that point—it doesn't go back to being only yours. It moves forward.

Your Thought

Finishing a first draft isn't about getting it right—it's about getting it done. It's the moment your story finally exists outside of you, no longer in pieces, but as something whole, even if it still needs work.

Carry This

When you reach the end, don't rush to fix it. Sit with it for a moment. Let the weight of finishing settle before you move into editing. The first draft doesn't need to be refined—it only needs to exist so you have something real to shape.

What Stayed

A first draft isn't finished. But it's no longer just an idea.

The Long Walk

By the time the book was finished, I thought the hardest part was over. The writing was done. The chapters had been shaped and reshaped until they finally held. I had stayed with it long enough to bring it to an end.

But finishing the manuscript didn't mean the process was finished. It meant something else was beginning.

The first time I opened KDP I stared at it the way I had stared at the blank page at the beginning — not knowing where to start, not knowing what the process actually required, not knowing how many steps were between me and a finished book. Writing had asked me to look inward. This asked me to learn something completely new from the outside in.

ISBN registration came first. A number I had to acquire before anything else could move forward. It seemed simple until it wasn't — forms, classifications, publisher information, fields I had never filled out before. I sat with it longer than I expected, reading instructions twice, making sure I understood what I was entering before I entered it.

Then came formatting. The manuscript I had written over months of late nights now had to be transformed into something a printing system could read and reproduce exactly. Page size. Margins. Font. Line spacing. Headers. Page numbers. Things I had never thought about while writing suddenly mattered in very specific ways. I used software I was learning while using it — adjusting, saving, opening the file again, finding something that had shifted, adjusting again.

Every night I found something. An alignment that was off. A page break that landed in the wrong place. A margin that looked right on screen and wrong in the preview. I would fix one thing and something else would move. I would correct the second thing and the first would shift again.

It was repetition. Night after night. Frustrating in a way that writing never was — because writing had emotion in it, memory in it, something I could feel moving. This felt like chasing a problem that kept changing shape.

Then came design. The cover I had worked on had to meet specific technical requirements – dimensions, resolution, spine width calculated precisely based on page count. I uploaded it and it was rejected. I recalculated and rebuilt and uploaded again. Rejected again. I sat there with cold coffee reading the error message, wondering if this was the part that would stop everything.

It wasn't. Third upload. It went through.

I did not celebrate. I exhaled and kept going.

Some nights I stepped away completely. Went into a bookstore – not to read, but to study. Margins. Spacing. The way chapters opened. The way pages felt in my hands. I was trying to understand something I had never been taught by looking at books that had already solved the same problems I was trying to solve.

Slowly, piece by piece, it started to make sense. Not because someone handed me a system. Because I stayed with it long enough to build one.

Each night I understood a little more than the night before. Each problem I solved taught me something the next problem required.

And when it finally came together — when the file uploaded cleanly, the preview showed pages that looked the way they were supposed to look, and the manuscript that had lived on my screen for months was suddenly a book that could be held — the satisfaction was unlike anything else.

Not the satisfaction of finishing a chapter. Something different. Something more solid.

Because this part required a different kind of work. Writing had asked me to feel. This asked me to persist. And persistence, repeated enough times across enough frustrated nights, had produced something real.

The story was still there. But now it was held inside something that could travel.

Your Thought

You don't need to know how to do everything before you begin. You need the willingness to learn it by doing it. Frustration is not a sign that you are doing it wrong — it is part of how you learn something you have never done before. Every problem solved becomes knowledge you carry forward.

Carry This

When the technical side feels overwhelming, break it into single steps. Learn one thing at a time. Return to it the next night with fresh eyes. What feels impossible the first time becomes familiar the third time. Stay with it the same way you stayed with the writing — consistently, patiently, and without expecting it to be easy.

What Stayed

The frustration was part of it. So was the satisfaction when it finally held.

Preparing the Manuscript

I thought finishing the writing meant the book was done — that once the last sentence was written, everything else would follow.

It didn't.

The story was there. The chapters were complete. But when I opened the manuscript again, something felt different.

It wasn't a book yet.

The words existed, but they weren't shaped into something that could live beyond the screen.

That's when I realized I had reached a different kind of work. It was no longer about remembering or writing. It was about building.

The first thing I did was scroll to the bottom of the manuscript to see the page count. I had been writing for so long, in so many sessions, that I had lost track of how much was actually there.

Three hundred and forty-five pages.

I read that number twice. Then I sat back in my chair and just looked at it.

I had carried all of that. Written all of that. Page by page, night by night, it had accumulated into something I could hold in my hands. That was the first moment the book felt real to me — not as a finished thing, but as a physical fact. Three hundred and forty-five pages existed that had not existed before I sat down and began.

That number changed how I looked at everything that came next.

I started noticing things I had ignored before — margins, page breaks, chapter placement. Small details that changed everything. Because now, it wasn't just about writing. It was about how the reader would experience it.

At first, it felt unfamiliar. I wasn't shaping scenes anymore — I was shaping how someone would move through them. I adjusted the pages, trying to make them feel steady and consistent, something that wouldn't shift every time I opened the file.

The manuscript had been alive while I was writing it, changing constantly. But now, it needed to hold its form.

That's when I saw it more clearly. This was no longer just my story. It was something someone else would hold. And that changed the way I looked at every detail.

I had never thought about the physical size of a book before. While writing, the page felt endless. Now I had to decide how it would exist in real space — how large the pages would be, how the words would sit inside them, how it would feel in someone's hands.

It seemed small, but it changed everything.

The pages tightened. The story shifted.

Then I noticed the margins. Space I had ignored before suddenly mattered. Without it, the words felt crowded, too close to the edge, like they didn't have room to breathe. Adjusting it didn't change the story, but it changed how it felt to read.

The empty space became part of the experience.

I moved through the manuscript again, this time paying attention to how it looked as much as what it said — the font, the spacing, the placement of each chapter. None of it was decoration. It was structure.

If it was done right, the reader wouldn't notice it. They would just move through the story.

Even the chapter titles changed in that stage. While writing, they were markers for me. Now they became part of the reader's rhythm — where they paused, where they entered something new, where the story shifted.

I started seeing the manuscript differently — not as something I was still working on, but as something I was preparing to release.

And then there was the table of contents. For the first time, I saw everything at once — not as separate chapters written over time, but as a full path. A beginning. A middle. An end.

That's when it became real in a different way.

Then the proof copy arrived.

I had been waiting for it at home, sitting in my lounge chair in the living room. When it came I set it on the table in front of me and looked at it for a moment before picking it up.

It was heavier than I expected.

Not by much. But enough that I noticed it — the weight of it in my hands, the solidity of something that had once existed only on a screen. I ran my thumb along the spine. The pages felt different than they ever had as a document. There was resistance to them, a quality that made them feel real in a way digital pages never do.

I opened to the first chapter. Read the first paragraph—my own words, set on a page, in a book, in my hands.

I had to sit down. I was already sitting — but something in me needed to settle with it.

I moved through it carefully, not as the writer, but as someone seeing it for the first time. Small details stood out — the way the pages sat, the way the chapters broke, the way it held.

The story was no longer just a record of what happened. It became something shared.

Your Thought

Writing the book is only part of the process. Preparing it is what allows it to become something real. The way it is structured and presented shapes how it is experienced, and when it is done well, the reader moves through it without ever noticing the work behind it.

Carry This

As you begin preparing your manuscript, shift your attention to how it feels as a whole. Notice the way chapters open, how the spacing settles, how the words sit on the page. Think about the person holding it, moving through it, and make choices that support clarity and ease rather than distraction.

What Stayed

A book isn't just written. It's built.

The Technical Maze

I thought I was done. The story was written. The chapters were shaped. I had gone through it enough times to feel like it finally held together the way it was supposed to.

All that was left, I thought, was turning it into a book.

That part felt simple in my head. The words were already there. How hard could it be to place them onto a page?

It wasn't simple.

The first thing I noticed was the outline. Not a writing outline — a formatting one. Dotted lines running through the manuscript in Microsoft Word, marking where pages broke, where sections divided, where the document had been making decisions I had never paid attention to while writing. I had ignored them for months. Now they mattered. Every one of them.

I started in Word because it was what I knew. But Word was not built for book formatting the way a book needs to be formatted. Things moved when I didn't ask them to. A paragraph would shift after I adjusted a margin. A page break would land in the wrong place after I changed the font size. I would fix one thing and something else would follow it — not randomly, but connected in ways I didn't fully understand yet.

Half page matters appeared everywhere. A chapter ending with three lines on a page that should have been full. A scene break landing awkwardly in the middle of a moment. These were not mistakes in the writing. They were decisions the formatting required — decisions I had to learn to make deliberately instead of letting the document make them for me.

I moved to Adobe InDesign. The learning curve was steeper but the control was real. I could see the pages the way a designer sees them — the space between lines, the weight of margins, the way text sat inside a page rather than just filling it. I had never thought about any of that while writing. Now it was all I could see.

That was when the cover became the problem.

I had designed it — front, back, spine — and uploaded it to KDP. The system rejected it. Spine width wrong. Not dramatically wrong. Just enough that the text would not sit where it was supposed to sit.

I sat there staring at the error message. Coffee going cold beside me. The cover I had spent weeks on, the image I had adjusted and refined and finally felt right about, was being rejected because of a measurement I had miscalculated by a fraction.

I went to Photopea — the design tool I had been using — and rebuilt the file using KDP's cover calculator, entering my exact page count to get the correct spine measurement. Recalculated everything. Adjusted the spine. Made sure the text cleared the edges. Uploaded again.

Rejected again.

I did not react out loud. I just sat with it. Read the error message again. Found the detail I had missed. Fixed it. Third upload.

It went through.

I did not celebrate. I exhaled and kept going.

Toward the end of the process I started going to Barnes and Noble. Not to browse. To study. I would walk through the shelves slowly, pulling books off and opening them — not to read the words but to look at the pages. How the margins sat. Where the chapter titles landed. How much white space surrounded the text. What the page count felt like in the hand. How the spine looked on a book that had been done right.

I was trying to understand something by looking at books that had already solved the problems I was still working through. Every book on that shelf had gone through the same process. Someone had made the same decisions I was trying to make. I just needed to see what those decisions looked like when they were finished.

By that point I was also writing another book. Life did not stop for the technical process any more than it had stopped for the writing. I would sit down at night, work through whatever the current formatting problem was, and then shift to new pages for the next manuscript. The two things existed side by side — the technical work of finishing one book and the early emotional work of beginning another.

That was its own kind of lesson. The process does not end. You finish one thing and something new is already beginning beside it.

But the technical maze did close. Not all at once — through repetition, through returning to it night after night, through learning each piece until it stopped being unfamiliar. What had once produced error messages and shifting margins and dotted lines I did not understand became something I could move through with confidence.

The story was still there throughout all of it. But now it depended on every surrounding detail being right. And making those details right required a completely different kind of patience than writing had ever asked for.

Writing asked me to feel. This asked me to persist.

Both were necessary. Neither was optional.

And when the file finally uploaded cleanly — when the preview showed pages that sat the way they were supposed to sit, margins that held, a spine that carried the title exactly where it belonged — the satisfaction was solid and quiet and entirely earned.

Your Thought

The technical side of publishing is not separate from the creative work — it is part of it. Every formatting decision shapes how the reader experiences the story. Learning it takes time and repetition, but what begins as frustrating becomes familiar, and what becomes familiar becomes something you own.

Carry This

When the technical process feels overwhelming, move through it one problem at a time. Learn the software by using it. Study finished books to understand what the decisions look like when they are done right. Return to it night after night the same way you returned to the writing — consistently, without expecting it to be easy, and with the understanding that each problem solved teaches you something the next one requires.

What Stayed

Every book on that shelf went through the same process. Yours just had to go through it too.

Covers, Titles & Identity

Long before the book physically existed, it already carried a shape in my mind.

Not the pages themselves.

The feeling of it.

I knew the story before I knew what the cover looked like, but eventually the book needed something outward-facing—something that could hold everything inside it without explaining too much.

That part took longer than I expected.

At first, titles came and disappeared quickly. Some sounded too broad once I saw them written down. Others explained too much. A few felt distant from the emotional center of the story itself.

I kept returning to the same question:

What does this book actually carry underneath everything else?

The answer was never only memory.

It was survival. Family. Displacement. Identity. The quiet persistence of roots surviving through separation and change.

That was where Resilient Roots finally came from.

Once the title settled into place, the rest of the identity around the book started becoming clearer too.

The cover mattered for the same reason.

I didn't want it to simply describe the story. I wanted it to feel connected to it emotionally before a single page was opened. Something restrained. Honest. Quiet enough to match the tone of the writing itself.

I spent a long time looking at covers differently after that.

Not as decoration.

As atmosphere.

I started noticing how certain books carried a feeling before you even touched the first page. The texture of the image. The amount of empty space.

The way a title sat across the cover without competing against itself.

I wanted my book to feel that way too.

Not loud.

Certain.

Some evenings I would place different versions of the cover side by side on the screen and stare at them longer than I realized, trying to understand why one felt honest while another felt constructed. The smallest adjustments changed everything. A darker tone. More empty space. Simpler typography.

Eventually, I stopped trying to make the cover impressive and started trying to make it truthful.

That changed the direction completely.

The same thing happened with chapter titles. During writing, they existed mostly as markers for me. But once the manuscript became a real book, I started seeing them as part of the reader's movement through the story.

A chapter title became an entrance.

A pause.

A shift in emotional direction.

I wanted the titles to feel clean enough that the reader could enter the next chapter without unnecessary explanation before it even began.

That stage taught me something I hadn't expected.

A book begins speaking long before the reader reaches page one.

The title speaks.

The cover speaks.

The spacing speaks.

Everything surrounding the story quietly prepares the reader for what they are about to enter.

And eventually, after enough revisions and second-guessing and late nights staring at different versions on the screen, the identity of the book finally settled into place.

Not because it became perfect.

Because it finally felt honest.

Your Thought

The visual identity of a book shapes the reader's experience before the story even begins. Titles, covers, typography, and design choices all communicate emotional tone quietly and indirectly. The strongest choices are often the ones that feel most aligned with the truth of the work itself rather than the ones trying hardest to attract attention.

Carry This

When choosing titles, covers, or design elements, focus less on impressing people and more on creating something emotionally aligned with the work itself. Pay attention to what feels honest to the tone of the story you've written. Often the simplest choices carry the strongest identity.

What Stayed

The book started speaking long before anyone opened the first page.

Publishing the Book

For a long time, the book stayed with me. On my screen. In my control. The chapters were written, revised, adjusted until the pages finally held the way they were supposed to.

Everything felt finished—but it wasn't a book yet. It still belonged to me.

Publishing didn't begin with something dramatic. It began with a screen.

I opened the platform and sat there for a moment, realizing how different this part was from everything that came before. Writing had been private. Editing had been controlled. Every change stayed with me.

This was different. Now the process was moving outside of me.

I created the account without much thought—a name, an email, basic details that didn't feel connected to the weight of what I had just finished. But something had already shifted. The story was no longer staying where I had kept it.

Uploading the manuscript was the first moment I felt it. I selected the file, watched it load, and waited as the system processed it. The same pages I had read over and over were now being checked, measured, placed into something I couldn't fully control anymore.

It wasn't just a document now. It was being treated like a book.

Then came the cover. Seeing it paired with the manuscript changed something again. What had lived as separate parts—words, title, image—was now one thing.

It looked finished, even before I held it. I saw it the way someone else would. And that stayed with me.

The steps continued, but they didn't feel small. Each one carried weight—details I had never thought about before. Even choosing the price felt unfamiliar. How do you measure something that didn't begin as a product? Something that took years to understand—and even longer to write?

There wasn't a clear answer. Just a number placed where one was required.

Then came the proof copy—the moment everything became real.

When it arrived, I set it on the kitchen table and looked at it for a moment before picking it up.

It was heavier than I expected.

Not by much. But enough that I noticed it—the weight of it in my hands, the solidity of something that had once existed only on a screen. I ran my thumb along the spine. The pages felt different than they ever had as a document. There was resistance to them, a quality that made them feel real in a way digital pages never do.

I opened to the first chapter. Read the first paragraph. My own words, set on a page, in a book, in my hands.

I had to sit down.

I moved through it carefully, not as the writer, but as someone seeing it for the first time. Small details stood out—the way the pages sat, the way the chapters broke, the way it held.

And once that was done, there was only one step left.

Publishing.

The button itself was small. Nothing about it matched the weight of everything that came before it, but I knew what it meant. It would move into places I couldn't see, into hands I didn't know.

I sat there for a moment before pressing it. Not because I wasn't ready, but because I understood what was about to change.

Then I did it.

And just like that—it was no longer only mine.

Your Thought

Publishing isn't just another step in the process—it's a shift. It's the moment your story moves from something held privately into something shared, from something you could return to and shape, into something that begins to exist beyond you.

Carry This

Move through the publishing process one step at a time, giving each part your full attention. Review carefully, adjust where needed, and allow yourself to feel the transition as it happens. This isn't just about uploading a file—it's about letting your work take its place in the world.

What Stayed

This is where your book leaves you.

Pressing "Publish"

The button was small. But the moment wasn't.

For a long time, the book belonged only to me. It lived on my screen, inside files I could open and close, on pages I could return to and change as many times as I needed. Every sentence had passed through my hands. Every chapter could still be adjusted.

Nothing was final. And that's what made it feel safe.

Even at the end, it still felt that way. The manuscript was finished. The cover was in place. Everything had been checked more times than I could count.

There was nothing left to fix. But it still hadn't left me.

That part didn't change until the very last step.

I remember sitting there with everything ready. The screen open. The button in front of me. Nothing missing. Nothing needing more work.

And still, I paused.

I hovered there longer than I expected, because I understood what came next.

Up until that point, the story had been mine to shape. I could return to any part of it, change it, adjust it, keep it as long as I needed before letting it go.

But once I pressed that button, that part would end.

The story would move beyond me.

That was the shift. Not in the work, but in the ownership of it.

I could feel everything in that moment—the weight of finishing it, the time it took to get there, and the quiet realization that I wouldn't be the only one inside it anymore.

I wasn't afraid of the writing. I had already faced that. I understood what it meant to release it.

There's no control after that. The story goes where it goes, meets people you'll never see, and is understood in ways you didn't plan.

None of that belongs to you anymore.

I sat there for a second longer.

Then I pressed it.

Nothing around me changed. The room stayed the same. The screen didn't shift in any dramatic way.

But I felt it. The story had moved. It was no longer something I was holding. It was something I had let go of.

And that was the final step.

Because what it took was never just one moment. It was everything that came before it—time that had to be made, not found; returning to the same pages again and again until they finally held; learning what I didn't know; continuing even when it didn't work the way I expected; staying with the parts that were difficult and writing them anyway; showing up when it was clear and when it wasn't; working through it when it moved forward and when it felt like it wasn't moving at all.

This is what it takes.

Not perfection. Not certainty.

But the willingness to stay with it long enough to turn it into something real—and then to let it go.

Your Thought

Every writer reaches this moment. It isn't the fear of writing—it's the weight of releasing. Once you let your work go, it no longer belongs only to you. You can't control where it goes, how it's read, or what it becomes in someone else's hands. Learning to accept that is part of finishing.

Carry This

Before you take the final step, pause long enough to see your work clearly. Not as something unfinished—but as something complete in its own way. Trust what you've created, let go of the need to control what happens next, and move forward without overthinking it. Finishing isn't about certainty—it's about being willing to release it.

What Stayed

You don't need certainty. You need courage.

PART V — The Garden

Letting Go

Writing a book feels deeply personal.

But once it is finished, something begins to shift. The story starts to move.

It no longer belongs entirely to you—and that is not a loss. It is the natural life of a story. What begins with a single voice, if it travels far enough, begins to speak in many.

When the book is finally published, it is easy to believe the journey is over. The pages are written, shaped, and printed. The long path from memory to manuscript has reached its end.

But the next morning looks the same.

The routines return. Coffee is poured. Work continues. Life does not pause.

That is the first surprise. Nothing around you changes.

The story, however, is no longer contained. It begins to move on its own, finding readers in ways you cannot see. Some come across it by accident. Others are led to it. You don't know when it happens or where it begins.

At first, there is a kind of quiet.

You expect something to happen right away—a response, a reaction, a sign that it has reached someone. But most of the time, nothing moves that quickly. The book exists somewhere beyond you, in places you cannot see, in hands you may never know.

Then, slowly, it happens.

A message arrives. A conversation begins. Someone recognizes a moment that felt like their own. Not always the one you expected—sometimes something smaller, something you almost overlooked.

A scene you wrote in solitude now exists in someone else's life.

That is when the distance disappears.

The story is no longer a record of what happened. It becomes something shared.

What began as a single memory, written quietly on a page, moves beyond you.

You are no longer the only one carrying it.

Readers do not follow the path you walked while writing it. They find their own way through it. They pause in different places. They carry different moments forward. What felt personal becomes something they recognize without knowing you at all.

The shift is not in the story itself—but in who is holding it.

Meaning is no longer fixed. It changes depending on who is reading. The pages stay the same, but the experience does not.

And that is when you understand it fully—the story no longer belongs to you.

Not because you lost it, but because it no longer needs you to carry it.

Writing the book was only one part. Letting it go is the other.

It means not controlling where it goes. Not needing to know who reads it. Not measuring its value by how quickly it moves. It means allowing it to exist—and trusting that it will reach the people it is meant to reach.

Because once the book leaves you, it begins a life you are no longer part of.

And that is where it becomes something more than what you wrote.

Because a story does not end when it is finished. It changes—when it is read.

Your Thought

Once your story is released, it no longer belongs only to you. It begins to shift, to take on new meaning through the people who experience it. What you wrote stays the same, but what it becomes continues to grow beyond you.

Carry This

Let your work exist without holding onto it. You don't need to follow where it goes or shape how it's received. Trust that it will find its way, and allow yourself to keep moving forward instead of looking back.

What Stayed

A story doesn't end when you finish it. It begins again—with someone else.

What Changes

People often ask what it feels like to finish writing a book. The question usually carries the assumption that the biggest change happens after publication—that something shifts once the story reaches readers.

But the deeper change happens earlier.

Writing a book quietly reshapes the writer.

While working on Resilient Roots, I spent hours returning to moments I had not examined in years. Memories that once lived in the background moved to the center—scenes from childhood, conversations, and experiences that had shaped my path.

At first, I believed I was only describing what had happened.

But as the pages grew, I began to understand it.

Events that once felt separate revealed their connections. A decision made years later could be traced back to something much earlier. Certain fears, strengths, and habits began to show where they came from.

Writing required a different kind of honesty. Not the kind we use in conversation, where difficult moments are softened—but a deeper honesty that does not turn away.

That part can be uncomfortable.

There are moments when the writer must face things that were easier left unexplored.

But those moments bring clarity. They reveal not only what happened—but how it shaped what followed.

While writing Resilient Roots, I began to see my life differently. What once felt like a series of events became something I could step back and understand as a whole. I could see the resilience that had been forming, even in moments when I had not recognized it.

The act of writing changed the way the past lived inside me.

A writer begins believing they are shaping a story. But the story shapes them as well.

The discipline of returning to the page, the courage required to stay inside difficult moments, and the patience needed to refine each chapter all leave their mark.

By the time the manuscript is complete, the writer is not the same person who began.

The story has not changed—but the way it is understood has.

And that becomes one of the lasting gifts of writing it.

Your Thought

Writing a book isn't only about telling a story—it's about coming to understand it. And somewhere in that process, the way you see it begins to shift. What once felt separate starts to connect, and in understanding the story more clearly, you begin to understand yourself differently as well.

Carry This

As you write, notice what begins to change. Pay attention to the connections that form over time, the patterns that quietly reveal themselves, and the moments that start to make sense in ways they hadn't before. Writing isn't only about putting something down—it's about discovering what was already there.

What Stayed

You don't finish writing the same person who started.

Every Story Has Roots

When I began writing Resilient Roots, I believed I was telling something that belonged only to me.

I didn't expect it to open the door to other people's stories.

But it did.

Again and again, after sharing parts of my journey, someone would say it quietly—

"I have a story too."

It was never said as a statement. More like something they had been holding for a long time.

And almost always, the same hesitation followed.

"I just don't know how to write it."

I understood that immediately. Before I began, I had thought the same thing.

Writing felt like something other people did—people who had studied it, people who knew where to begin.

HALAINA

I wasn't thinking about writing a book. I was carrying a life I hadn't yet put into words.

And that's where every story begins.

Not on the page—but inside the person who lived it.

Most stories are not missing. They are waiting.

People remember more than they realize. A moment. A place. A voice. Something small that stays.

That's where the story lives.

You don't begin with everything. You begin with one piece. Then another. That's how it takes shape—not all at once, but honestly.

The roots are already there.

They hold what came before, even when it hasn't been spoken.

And once it begins, it has a way of continuing. Not because the writer knows exactly how to do it—but because the story does.

Your Thought

Every story begins long before it's written. It lives quietly in the moments that stay, in the memories that return without being called. The challenge isn't finding something to say—it's allowing yourself to begin.

Carry This

Pay attention to what comes back to you without effort. A place, a voice, a moment that hasn't left. Start there. Don't try to shape it into something complete—just let it exist as it is. Write it simply, without pressure, and allow it to lead you forward one piece at a time.

What Stayed

Every story has roots. Yours is already there.

What Remains

By the time you reach the end, something has already settled. It doesn't happen all at once, and not always in a way that can be explained, but it's there—an understanding that stories don't begin on the page. They begin long before that, in moments that stay, in memories that return, and in things that were never said out loud but were never forgotten.

Writing gives those moments a place to exist outside of the person who carries them.

When I began writing Resilient Roots, I thought I was recording what had happened—placing memories on a page so they wouldn't be lost. But the deeper work wasn't memory. It was truth. Not perfect recall or every detail exactly as it was, but the honesty of what it felt like to live it.

That's what gives a story weight.

It was never about what the book would become or how many people would read it. It was about telling the story the way it lived inside me, without softening it.

Some parts were harder to write than others—not because I didn't remember them, but because I understood what it meant to put them on the page. There are moments where you have to decide what matters more: comfort or truth.

I chose truth. And that is the hardest part.

Some moments are easy to return to. Others ask you to stay longer than you want to, to look at them without turning away. That's where a story either holds or weakens, because readers recognize truth—not just in what is said, but in how it is told.

They feel when something has been softened. And they feel when it hasn't.

That is what allows a story to move beyond you.

A moment you lived begins to exist in someone else—not exactly as it was, but in a way that meets them where they are. And from there, it continues. That's the part no writer controls. Once it is read, the story changes hands. It grows in ways you will never see.

What began as something private doesn't stay contained. It moves outward.

Writing doesn't require perfection. It asks for something else—the willingness to stay inside what is true, even when it isn't easy to hold. That's where a story takes shape. Not in order, and not all at once, but piece by piece.

Some parts come easily. Others resist—and those are often the ones that matter most. They ask you to slow down, to stay longer than you planned, and to write what you might have once avoided.

Over time, something changes.

The story becomes clearer—not because it has been perfected, but because it has been faced honestly. And in that process, you change too. What once felt scattered begins to make sense. What once felt heavy begins to settle.

Eventually, the story reaches a point where it can be released—not finished in perfection, but finished in truth. And once it is released, it no longer stays where it began.

It moves. It meets people you will never see. It is understood in ways you didn't plan. And it continues—without you.

Writing the book changed me. Not just because I finished it, but because I stayed with it. Through doubt. Through uncertainty. Through everything that tried to stop it.

And in the end, it became something real.

That is what remains.

Not just the story—but the understanding that it was always there, waiting to be told.

Your Thought

You don't just write a book—you become someone who finishes one. And that change doesn't disappear when the last page is done. It stays with you, shaping how you see your work, your voice, and what you're capable of creating next.

Carry This

Take a moment to recognize what this process has changed in you. Not just what you've written, but what you've learned by staying with it. Let that growth carry you forward. Don't wait too long to begin again—momentum builds when you continue, even after something this significant is complete.

What Stayed

You didn't just write a story. You proved you could.

About the Author

Halaina is the author of Resilient Roots, Rooted in Truth, One Land, Two Sides, and Miles From Home.

A mother of four, entrepreneur, and salon owner, she rebuilt her life after abuse, betrayal, and financial loss—emerging not hardened, but grounded.

Her story spans continents and crossroads—from Ramallah to Myrtle Beach, from broken marriages to restored family bonds. Through faith and perseverance, she reclaimed what once seemed lost.

She lives in South Carolina, where she owns a salon, travels alone in a motorhome, and writes the truth she once had no words for.

Stay Connected

halaina.com

For new releases, book updates, and contact information.

www.ingramcontent.com/pod-product-compliance
Lightning Source LLC
LaVergne TN
LVHW090524110826
845146LV00003B/975

* 9 7 9 8 9 9 4 5 3 6 7 2 8 *